S.

MW01245007

Fifteen Life Lessons for College

Emily Hepp

outskirts
press

She Is More Than The Freshman Fifteen
Fifteen Life Lessons for College
All Rights Reserved.
Copyright © 2017 Emily Hepp
v4.0

The opinions expressed in this manuscript are solely the opinions
of the author and do not represent the opinions or thoughts of the
publisher. The author has represented and warranted full ownership
and/or legal right to publish all the materials in this book.

This book may not be reproduced, transmitted, or stored in
whole or in part by any means, including graphic, electronic, or
mechanical without the express written consent of the publisher
except in the case of brief quotations embodied in critical articles
and reviews.

Outskirts Press, Inc.
http://www.outskirtspress.com

ISBN: 978-1-4787-8739-6

Cover Photo © 2017 Emily Hepp. All rights reserved - used with
permission.

Outskirts Press and the "OP" logo are trademarks belonging to
Outskirts Press, Inc.

PRINTED IN THE UNITED STATES OF AMERICA

Dedicated to my friends and family who have been important in all the lessons of my life and believed in more.

Table of Contents

INTRODUCTION

She Is More Than The
Freshman Fifteen

She is more than her high school. She is more than her token nickname given to her as a child. She is more than the stereotypical clique she was assigned. She is more than her class ranking. She is more than whom she dated. She is more than where she sat in the cafeteria. She is more than the style of clothes she wore and the car she drove. She is more...and she will be more than the freshman fifteen.

Wait, what did I just sign myself up for? Hello, it's me. "Me," as in every soon-to-be college girl, who on the outside is as calm as a cucumber, but on the inside is mentally freaking out about what is to come. My name is Emily and I have been in your shoes. Unfortunately, I don't have the master key to unlock all of the secret codes of everything college, but I have been through it and walked off with my diploma feeling proud, excited, and even nostalgic. Quite frankly, I am also secretly, or not so secretly, ready to go back to the world filled with class schedules allowing me to frolic with friends around campus whenever I choose and stay up until 2 a.m. watching wedding proposals on YouTube with my roommates. Jumping from college to college to college from state to state to state, I began to learn a whole lot about the world of colleges in a quick amount of time. Yes, if you're following along, I attended three different colleges within the time span of my freshman/sophomore year alone.

Disclaimer: Not highly recommended if at all possible.

Without all of these different life changes, multiple roommates, polar opposite climates, and millions of phone calls to Mom, I wouldn't be sitting here today feeling the need to write this book. I truly hope this book brings you peace, calms your nerves, and gets you excited for some of the best years of your life! I have always had a passion for inspiring young women and felt as though I could have used a "cheat sheet" myself as I entered the sometimes crazy world of college. So, I decided to write a book. I may not be a world-renowned journalist, I don't work for a major magazine (#dreamjob), and I'm not a famous celebrity, BUT what I do know is that I am a normal girl who has been there and wants to be there for you, too. Let's take a twist on the "freshman fifteen" and cover fifteen college lessons to empower your next chapter in life. No scales needed! Now, get out your way too cute, personalized planner and let's begin with lesson one.

LESSON #1

Speed Dating
Roommate & Housing Edition

Are you a train wreck when it comes to your room or does the sight of unorganized chaos send you into an anxiety attack? Do you prefer an extroverted roommate who won't pass up a single social opportunity or an introverted roommate who can be located on the comfiest couch under the blanket with take-out? How do you feel about co-ed sleepovers, awkward but a necessary question? Do you fall asleep with your favorite playlist on or do you like to sleep in the cave of darkness in complete silence? Are you looking to room with someone that you are already besties with or go pot-luck? Are you thinking to yourself what does a cooking pot and some luck even have to do with one another, yet alone with housing? Well, then you're in the right lesson.

Whew! Do you feel like you are going through a speed dating exercise? I know that I did when the day comes around where you have to make those what seem like "life decisions" that will affect your entire freshman year. Have no fear. I just might have a close "friend" of mine who has fortunately and unfortunately been through about every rooming situation there was to offer as a freshman. Let's be real here, that person was me. I have personally lived in a suite that included eight women with a shared community living space. Add to that situation, we all had roommates through the potluck system. If you're still wondering what in the world that term even means, I promise I will fill you in soon. Then I moved back to the Midwest and lived in a similar setting, had a room to myself, and had a room-mate who was potluck, whom I shared a common bathroom and living area. Next, I moved into a "sophomore" living community that resembled the looks of a nice hotel where I shared a room with another potluck decision for an entire year.

Yahoo, I successfully lived somewhere for a full year (this was a big accomplishment for me at the time). I then did the whole commuting route where I lived with my parents, located about thirty minutes away from my campus. Last, but certainly not least, I spent my final semester living in an off campus house with two of my closest friends. I'm exhausted just talking about my experiences, but I am #blessed that I have experienced all of these living situations. It puts me in a much better place to go over the pros and cons of each experience to help guide your way in what may seem like one of the biggest decisions of your freshman year.

Potluck vs. Pre-Selected Roommate(s) – (Standard Dorm Room)

For those of you who have not yet heard of this terminology, potluck does not involve reaching into a large pot to randomly select a name that you will live with for the remainder of your next ten months. Well, now that I think of it, maybe it is? Potluck is when you do not know who your roommate will be and the campus randomly assigns you a roommate based on what seems like a never-ending questionnaire. My advice is to actually spend time filling out your roommate request. Be brutally honest, they actually do read these and take them seriously. Most colleges also offer you the option to pre-select your roommate, if you already know of a friend or potential bestie attending the same college. May the potluck odds be ever in your favor (prayers to the roomie gods – insert hands up praise emoji for some extra luck).

Pros - Potluck: First things first, by selecting potluck, I want you to know that you took a leap of faith and I am so proud of you. It takes a lot of courage to choose this route, no matter what the outcome. Throughout my different roommate scenarios, I found that no matter what, I learned something about myself or about someone else, which I may have never encountered on my own. Going potluck may involve some Facebook creeping, and a slight sense of anxiety, but it also can be life-changing. When I landed at my final college, I decided to go potluck since I knew literally no one. When I say no one, I mean not a single soul, not even a friend of a friend of a friend (not even a random acquaintance of my Aunt's twice removed cousin who made her way to the West Coast). You get the picture. I still to this day thank the

Lord above for blessing me with one of the best potluck roommates and lifelong friends I could have ever imagined. Yes, we may have had completely opposite styles and personalities, but it didn't matter. I still laugh looking back remembering me moving into our dorm before her with my all pink polka dot bedding and white ruffled rug and her first comment being, "Wow, you sure like the color pink." At the end of the day, I was privileged to meet someone who made me a better person, laughed with me until late hours of the night, and cried with me on our little shared bedroom floor, while she made hot chocolate. To think that I would have most likely never have met her if I didn't go potluck literally brings tears to my eyes because she was my angel when I needed one the most. Thank you, Allison!

Cons – Pre-Selecting Roommate: Why meet new people when you already have your bestie as a roommate from high school? I totally get it! It's comfortable, you don't have to worry about offending them, and you've probably already got your color palette picked out for your dorm. My only word of caution with choosing to pre-select your roommate is that it may limit you from meeting new people on campus. It's almost like having a security blanket with you at all times. This can be both good and bad for some people. If you do decide this route, I encourage you to have conversations with your roommate beforehand about branching out and expanding your friend group. You don't want to appear closed off if you only hang out with your roomie.

Throughout my experiences, I have learned that just because you are best friends with some-one and can practically spend forty-eight hours with them without getting annoyed, it doesn't always mean that you are best suited to live with them. I've had many friends that I spent countless hours with on the weekend, but I just knew in my heart that living together could po-tentially ruin our friendship. I have seen it hap-pen so many times, especially with friends from high school. I would hate for you to risk los-ing a friendship over a living situation. My best friend in college lived three houses down from me during my senior year. I could walk over to her house as many times as I wanted, but we still had our own space and set of friends. It was the ideal option for us because it allowed room for growth. Not saying you can't live with your high school bestie, but please just be aware of potential outcomes!

Suite Style Living
(Multiple Girls Sharing a Suite)

Pros: There is never a shortage of friends to hang out or go grab a meal with and you are immediately thrown into a group of girls that are ready to mingle at a campus event. All my extroverts out there often times love this constant sleepover with some of your best friends.

Can you say #squadgoals? Living in this setting encourages many *Bachelor* nights, dance parties, and constant support from your tribe. Just think, you already have your dream team set for the next dorm floor competition. Someone bring out the obstacle course, it is game time ladies!

Cons: How many half-eaten pizza boxes can be left in the fridge? How many girls can fit in one bathroom to get ready for a night on the town? With this lifestyle, having shared areas with multiple people can cause quite the mess at times, the environment is not always conducive for a quiet study area, and your roommates may invite their friends over in your already cramped space. I probably wouldn't recommend this to my introverts out there. You may go slightly insane.

Suite Style Living
(Single Bedroom, Shared Living Space)

Pros: Are you the type of person who thrives on having "me" time at the end of each day? If so, this may be the option for you. The single bedroom is great for studying, alone time, and the opportunity to create a space that is right for your lifestyle. With this suite style, it allows you to be social and have a roommate, but on your own schedule. No more worrying about color schemes or matching pillows with your roommate. The room is all yours to decorate. Time to bring out your inner Joanna Gaines (minus the shiplap - may cause you some additional fees at dorm room check-out)!

Cons: How do you feel about awkwardly sharing a living room and bathroom with someone who may not be your future bridesmaid? For me, I moved into this scenario halfway through my freshman semester and was placed with a random or as they say potluck roommate. We had different personalities and little in common, so I found myself feeling awkward and staying in my room most of the time. If you happen to already know your roommate, then I feel as though it could be a much better situation. If you tend to feel lonely when not surrounded by people, this situation may leave you feeling isolated.

Dorm Room Hacks

Typically, most standard college dorm rooms include two desks, two chairs, two beds (possibly bunk beds), tight closet space, and some windows. Yes, probably the size of your bedroom at home, but adding an additional person with you. Some of you are already stressed out just thinking about it. No better time to get to know your roommate but in a tight space, am I right? Good news is that everyone else is in this together with you, so embrace the experience! It is one of a kind. I would discuss with your roommate beforehand if you would like to add a futon or small couch, especially if you loft or raise your beds. It provides additional seating and they are relatively cheap to purchase. Futons are ideal for when your high school best friend comes to visit you and needs a place to crash.

Let's just say goodbye for now to walk-in closets and hello to shared shelving! Try and bring your clothes for each season, instead of packing in all four seasons at once. A great time to trade out your clothes is during your holiday breaks. Added perk about the college schedule

– you typically have classes either Monday/Wednesday/Friday or Tuesday/Thursday. So, you better believe that you can rock the same shirt two days in a row if you need to because your Tuesday/Thursday classmates don't need to know about your Monday/Wednesday/Friday life. Just please do us all a favor and wash your clothes somewhat regularly. *Laundry Tip* - sheets need to be washed **more than once** a semester, students somehow tend to forget this much needed tip.

I know you have maybe heard horror stories about the dreaded community dorm bathrooms. Haven't we all! No, community bathrooms are not going to kill you (well, maybe if you don't take my flip-flop advice seriously in the next paragraph), but I would advise you to figure out the best time of day for your schedule to take a shower. Invest in a robe or bath towel wrap that you feel comfortable walking through the dorm halls and also a shower caddy, this lifesaver stores all your bathroom essentials in one place. Genius! I actually still use one today (slightly weird, I know), some college things just stick with you I guess, who knew! These bathrooms are located on the same floor as your dorm room, so luckily you won't be trekking too far. *Roll Call* - Just a word for the wise, fire alarms will go off at the most inconvenient times (for example: while in the middle of your shower), so be ready with your bathrobe at ALL times.

Now that we have covered all things roommates and housing, let's address the common problem of...college checklists. From popular magazines, to blogs, to movies, checking off EVERY item on the so-called "must-haves" for college is something we need to address. Yes, there are some very useful items to bring to college on this list including: bathrobe, comforter, sheets, laundry hamper, and the most important item, flip-flops. Yes, you will be very sorry if you forget flip-flops for the dorm showers. VERY SORRY. The other dorm must-have that I strongly recommend is purchasing a protective mattress cover and pad (or five) to place on top of that lovely, hard as rock, bed of yours.

Just ask yourself, do you really think that you will ever use the retractable shelving unit that turns into a locker for your dorm? I know that the dorm aisle is very tempting before you begin college. My advice would be to first get your essential items for living in your dorm. *Less is more*. I know some of you just won't be able to resist the matching lamps and mirrors, so how about you splurge with your summer money on one or two fun items to add to your collection? If you have the mentality that you can always add items when needed, this will keep your costs low and help you from overstocking your room. You want your new friends to be able to hang out in your room, not feel like they are in an overcrowded dorm advertisement.

One of the biggest "aha" moments that I had while living in the dorm was this simple statement. A closed door = closed opportunities. Now, this may sound slightly creepy at first, but when you close your dorm room door, it limits you from meeting new potential friends, especially at the beginning stages of college. Now, please shut your door while sleeping and when studying, no one wants to see you drooling with your childhood stuffed animal. Trust me. Most welcoming people keep their doors open. This allows you to interact with friends on your dorm floor and opens up numerous opportunities for social gatherings, binge watching parties, and endless Pinterest nights.

Quick Dorm Room Hacks - Loft your bed if at all possible to ensure a lot more storage, organize your clothes vertically in your drawers to create more space, place a car vent clip on your fans or vents to fill your room with crisp smelling air freshener, invest in a portable charger for times when you won't be returning to your room all day, label your chargers with your name on colorful tape to distinguish your pile of cords, create a vision board that is always in your view with all your semester goals to keep you accountable and inspired, purchase christmas lights to create a cozier looking room, and place a frozen water bottle in front of your fan for those hot, stuffy summer days to cool you off. With these dorm room hacks, you will be on your way to a better living situation!

Check your mail frequently. It's basically like Christmas morning every time you receive a slip that you have a package waiting for you. In order to receive these sometimes life-changing packages, be sure to send out your new mailing address to all your favorite family members (especially those who send treats or cash).

Bulletin Post: Did you know?

You will quickly hear of the term, RA, the minute you step into the dorms. RA stands for Resident Assistant and they are trained leaders who supervise students living in the residence halls or housing on campus. Basically, each hall has its own RA assigned to a specific floor. They will be in charge of organizing dorm floor activities and friendly competitions throughout the year. RAs will hold mandatory meetings every so often to go over general guidelines, updates, and discuss upcoming events on your floor. There will also be optional gatherings that you can attend. I would suggest that you attend at least the first few dorm activities. It is a great way to get to know your peers on your floor. You will be with them for the entire year, why not take time to get to know your neighbors? I advise you to get to know your RA! They are upperclassmen that have been in your shoes and their sole job is to educate, support, and be there for you! Think of them as your mentor. They are there as a resource to pretty much everything, from roommate issues to best study practices to health issues. It is similar to having an older sibling just a few steps away, which is the best feeling ever.

LESSON #2

Squad Goals

Close your eyes and picture yourself back in high school. For some of you, you may be like… "Emily, I'm still in high school, I don't have to close my eyes to picture it. I just want out of here." For others, high school brings back the good ol' days or those two words are words that you hope to permanently remove from your mind. Well, no matter which way you viewed those days of cliques, Friday night lights, and proms, I have some good news for you. One of the biggest changes that I noticed from high school to college is this…for once you are not defined by where you sit at the cafeteria, what parking lot you park in, or being annoyed that you grew up with these same people since first grade. BEST NEWS EVER! So that means that no one will remember when I had pink eye at prom and it was locally televised for everyone to see? Yes, we had this television program called *Prom TV*. Long story short, be glad you didn't have it! College frees you of this once and for all, thank goodness. Yes, you may join organizations, athletics, sororities, but don't let them "define" you, this is the time to make as many friends in as many groups because...guess what...you can!

Speaking of meeting new friends, now hear me out on this one. Freshman Orientation may sound SUPER corny and lame and silly and awkward...BUT everybody has got to go through it and it is the perfect solution to meet some friends from day one! You also don't want to be that one freshman without your campus map. Bad idea. By this I mean, as much as you may not want to grace them with your presence due to the thoughts above, there are actual benefits to attending. You get free food, free college gear, funny stories, and may even meet a friend or two who are also laughing with you about the lame "get to know your neighbor" game where you had to awkwardly race to the end of the field wearing the same oversized pair of sweatpants. Did you catch the overall theme - free, free, free? Trust me, you will appreciate this later, *anything free*. During orientation, you basically receive a private campus tour, the perfect way to find your classes ahead of time and will make you appear less "freshman" like on your first day. If you had thoughts of skipping orientation, you may want to rethink and change your attitude to being more open about this event. I know you want that free college hat and cute tumbler! Hey, you may even meet your lifelong partner at Freshman Orientation and can look back ten years from now on when you split that pretzel in the Commons. Can you say #relationshipgoals?

Personally, if I could create my own #squad, I would make sure to include Emma Stone, Carrie Underwood, Alexis Jones, Alicia Keyes, Becca Tilley, and Reese Witherspoon. A combination of influential women from all walks of life. One of the biggest takeaways from college was how fortunate I was to make all different types of friends. I want you to know that friendships take time and effort. I met my best friend, Jamie, a few months into college. Don't stress if you haven't met your person yet. They are out there waiting for you, too.

My own personal advice is to make at least one friend in the following categories: your designated bookworm (who keeps you focused and locked in the library), your go-to workout warrior (CrossFit is calling your name), your adventure is out there *Dora the Explorer* (the only one you would voluntarily join on a five mile hike), your necessary ugly-cry chick flick companion (sweats and face masks required), a trendy shopping buddy (aka your retail therapist), and the ever so important, life of the party girlfriend (who will pick out your outfit and drag you out the door). For me, I found a friend or two in each of these categories and I was so thankful. Please don't limit yourself to only one friend group or your #squad. It is always nice to have that bond with that certain group, but be open to those friends that come your way in class, that you meet at workouts, or the ones that you keep running into at the cafeteria. If you only have one friend group, you are limiting yourself to all of the possibilities at college. Doesn't that remind you of high school all over again? No thank you!

Can we please just take a moment to discuss the popular phrase "ride or die" when referring to our close friends? I'm just so fascinated with this phrase and always wonder these thoughts; can someone just please explain to me where we are going, do I need to bring snacks, is dying involved, and will there be restroom breaks? Any help appreciated.

LESSON #3

Declaring Your Major

True or False? Declaring your major is greater than or equal to declaring your career path for the rest of your life? You know that dreaded question that most of us always hate getting asked? "Oh, hi Emily, nice to meet you, just curious, what do you want to do with your life?" Okay, I'm being a bit dramatic, but sometimes it feels like this question can weigh you down SO much. This is a VERY commonly asked phrase when you are about to graduate high school and I hate to break it to you, but it will reappear throughout all of college. Lucky you! Most of the time I answer by saying, "Oh, you know, I would just like to save the planet, secure world peace, and leave a positive footprint on society." Oh wait. Am I supposed to leave a footprint? Is that now considered a bad thing? Now, I'm even more confused. Let's just go back to the main topic. The one thing that I have learned from the academic perspective of college is that the statement above is both true AND false. Yes, it is nice to know a direction of where you see yourself heading for your career field, but I also want you to know that choosing your major in college does not mean that you cannot switch career paths or even start in a different field after college. Now, it may be more costly if you decide to switch from your Communications major to Nursing after your second year of college, but I hope you are seeing the bigger picture.

Now, I know this can be hard to imagine, but picture yourself in what I think is the "happiest place on earth" - Target. Honestly, if guys only knew that the perfect date night would be strolling hand in hand through the endless aisles of Target, they would be saving a whole lot of money on expensive dinners. Am I right? The only problem that I have with Target is these three words – the dollar section. Every time it gets me. Do I need the adorable floral locker mirror that reads, "be present?" Of course I do! I'm pretty sure I am twenty-five years old and don't own a locker, but it's only a dollar! YOLO. Sold, to the lady with now an almost full shopping cart when she was only going in for two items.

You're probably thinking, where are you going with this? Well, I like to compare the wonderful world of Target to the career search. You've got the produce section, the endless makeup aisles, the adorable living section, and if it's that time of year, the tempting holiday candy aisle. Well, similar to the numerous aisles of choices, there are so many career options out there and opportunities to choose from, that sometimes it can become overwhelming. By setting aside some alone time to write down your passions, interests, and simply things that bring joy to your life, you will be on the right track to figuring out your destined career path. Now, all this talk about shopping has me wanting to go to Target. Who's with me? Meet you in the dollar section.

Do you picture yourself in the Television Industry, Public Relations, Pharmaceuticals, Performing Arts? Have you watched all thirteen seasons of *Grey's Anatomy* and feel as though you now know enough to diagnose your friends? You may believe that you are ready to take on the medical field as your next career move. Anyways, the list goes on and on. Within your freshman and sophomore year of college, you are pretty much expected to know which major and even minor that you would like to select and dedicate your time to this field. When I jumped around colleges, I also jumped around majors. I went from Hospitality and Tourism to Education to Communications with a minor in Leadership Studies. At that point, I could not have told you that I would end up working at a corporate headquarters for an airline after college, but I could have told you the following; I enjoy working with people, am interested in leadership development, and thrive in event planning. I decided on my own that I would rather have a broader major than one that kept me limited to a single career path. I knew that with a Communications major my career could go a variety of ways. I could become an Executive Assistant, Event Planner, Human Resource Representative, Marketing Executive, etc. The options were limitless for me, which I absolutely love to this day.

My point being, I want you to realize that at the time, it does seem like a life-changing decision (which it can be), but I also want you to know that it can be so exciting. Take this time to listen to your calling, try out your different passions, and with time, you will begin to see your career path unfold for itself. Take advantage of your Academic Advisor and lean on them to help decipher which route would be best for you to take for your chosen major and minor. Some students will have their "calling" and major figured out even before they begin their first day in college and others will not. I always was slightly intimidated by my older brothers because they both knew from pretty much childhood what they wanted to be when they were older. How annoying! One wanted to be an Entertainment Editor and the other an Animator. Meanwhile, I was just over here twiddling my thumbs and could barely decide where I wanted to go for dinner, how could I even begin to think about what I wanted to do for the rest of my life? I have learned that it does not make you behind or less driven, it just means that your career path may lead you in a few different directions at first, but those choices will ultimately guide you to your destined career over time.

Career Update

My two amazing brothers, Andrew and Austin, have both achieved their dream jobs and more. Way to go brothers, I'm still deciding where I want to go to eat...

LESSON #4

It's All Greek to Me

Is joining a sorority the right fit for me? The start of college is often times quite overwhelming. You are adjusting to being away from your hometown and parents, trying to meet new friends, figuring out how to live with someone you may have never met before, and on top of all of this, your fifteen hour course load is staring you down. The pyramid of life is building rapidly and you are just trying to make your way to the top, without losing too much sleep. Then, you are a few weeks (or halfway, depending on your college) into classes and you start hearing the rumblings of the word, recruitment.

Recruitment or rush are terms used in colleges referring to the process in which different chapters of sororities host you to their events to see if you could potentially be interested in joining their sorority. Before you know it, the booths are up, the Greek shirts are out, and it is time to decide whether or not Greek life is for you.

First and foremost, I want you to know that your college experience will not be defined by whether or not you are wearing Greek letters. I repeat…Greek letters do not define you in college and you should not let them. Your college experience is defined by how YOU shape it to be. For some girls, they will define their college experience by the internships and education that they received. Some will say that it was the multiple organizations that they were a part of and the friends that they made through those interactions. My goal in this lesson is to inform, educate, and provide real life examples of women who have experienced life in a college sorority and offer advice for those who did not go that route, but still had an amazing and memorable college experience.

To be 100% honest, I was a so-called "sorority girl" in college. My path led me to a sorority that I was honored and proud to be a member. At my college, this sorority was known for their academics and philanthropic work. These were two of my top qualities that were important to me in a sorority. I actually went through the recruitment process twice (almost three times). One was at a large state school and one a small private school. I had two completely opposite experiences with both of these recruitments. It is crucial to remember that each college has a different vibe, as well as different chapters. Each national sorority has individual chapters of their organization at different colleges and universities. It is important to understand that one chapter can be viewed with a certain reputation at one college, but be completely different at another college.

Please keep in mind that this is ultimately your decision. Your friends may start to influence you or even your family members. I went into recruitment as a triple legacy for one particular sorority. This meant that my Great Grandma, Grandma, and Aunt were all in this same sorority. Talk about pressure. Ultimately, it benefited me if I wanted to be in that sorority, but the overall vibe at that particular sorority (at that college) just wasn't for me. Yes, I was worried about hurting my family's feelings, but I knew in my heart that another sorority was a better fit for me. Hey, you may even say that the whole Greek thing isn't for you and that is perfectly okay, too! At the end of the day, just be yourself and please don't try to be someone that you are not. It will sadly only hurt you in the end.

Already having sorority stress just reading this? Images of matching t-shirts, girls chanting loudly with songs you don't understand, and trying to comprehend the Greek alphabet haunting your dreams? I promise you every girl going through this process feels the same as you at one point or another. I am here to tell you that everything will be okay, trust me and trust in the process. I want you to know that I could write a whole other book on this topic alone, but this lesson will provide you with just a brief overview of some tips and suggestions for the recruitment process. There will be resources on Greek life to pick up during your first few weeks of school that will include all that you need to know regarding proper attire, costs, and schedules. Deep breaths my friends, deep breaths.

How-To Guide of Greek Recruitment

1. Be Yourself.

I know it sounds cliché and out of yet another motivational Instagram post, but please, please, please try and be yourself. I know that this can be hard to do when you want to "fit in" with the most popular or loved sorority on campus. I promise you that it may seem cool at the time, but you will later regret your decision down the road. I knew when I walked into my sorority during recruitment and after interacting with a handful of women, that it was the right sorority for me. Emphasis on the word - *me*. Not for my Grandmother who was a legacy for another chapter, not for my best friend that I couldn't imagine not being together in the same sorority, not for the stereotype I heard from the other girls in my rush group. It was the right fit for *me*. It was where I felt the most comfortable and honestly in the end, that is all that matters. We talked about our mutual love for Luke Bryan, Galentine's Day, and you can't forget the never-ending adoration for Taco Tuesdays. Some of my other conversations at different sororities just didn't feel right to me. Everyone is looking for a different experience and outcome from Greek life, make sure you choose the right fit for you.

Side Note - Please don't use the word, "basic," to describe yourself. You are *anything but basic*, remember that.

2. Make a Recruitment Buddy.

One of the best parts of the recruitment process was honestly getting to know the girls in your rush group. You are randomly assigned to a small group of ladies for visiting each sorority, called your rush group. I am still friends with many of the girls I met during this process, even though most of them joined different sororities. I promise you that these girls are sharing the same feelings as you. Try and reach out to one or more girls that you get along with in your group and be that source of support for them, too.

3. Utilize your Rho Gammas.

Rho Gammas are ladies from all different sororities that will make up your mentors, guides, and resources throughout the entire recruitment process. They are hand selected from a competitive pool of applicants to be there for you as your support. You will not know which sorority they are members of until the final day, which allows you to be completely honest and open. When you are feeling lost, confused, excited, nervous, anxious, please utilize your Rho Gammas to talk to about your feelings. They are just as excited, nervous, and anxious for you because they have been there, too. They have felt the same emotions and they, too, leaned on their Rho Gammas when they went through recruitment. Please don't ask them which sorority they are in, they are not allowed to tell you which makes reveal day even more exciting! Another added bonus, you will forever have an instant mentor on campus even after this process is over, score!

4. Trust the Process.

In the final round, please *trust your instincts*. I remember walking into the room to sign my bid card (card received revealing your top sorority choices) and still not knowing which sorority I was going to choose. When it came down to it, I realized that one sorority stood out to me more because

I realized those girls were the ones that felt like long lost best friends and most importantly, I was 100% myself with them. That my friend, is key. Almost all of my friends who went through recruitment came out years later saying how they might not have known it at the time, but that sorority was the right fit for them for different reasons. Please give the sorority a try for the first few weeks. Every girl's experience will be different and it is important to remember to try and trust the process.

5. Try & Have Fun!

If a sorority ends up being the right fit for your college experience, try and remember to have fun throughout the process. Yes, it can be draining and you may feel like you can't talk to anyone else about your hometown, family, spirit animal or hobbies ever again, or you may explode! I have been there. Also keep in mind how many friends

you are making just during the recruitment process. Be proud of yourself
no matter the outcome because YOU
stepped outside of your comfort zone
and experienced a new environment
with brand new people, now that is
something to smile about. Just know
that you are truly amazing. I believe in
you and I also believe that this process
can be fun with the right approach!

What better way to find out more about recruitment than from a girl who has been there,
too. This dear friend of mine, Ellen, attended
college in the Midwest and has her own story
to share about the world of Greek life. Let's
take a listen in…

*When I found out the dates of rush, I began
getting nervous just thinking about it. My parents
weren't Greek but my sister went Greek and as
many people say, "met all of her bridesmaids and
her best friends for life." The movies always make
it out to be so awful and catty. I would tell anyone*

who asked me to just try. Greek life gives you a sense of "home" and "community" when are trying to find yourself in this new stage of life. It's full of driven, motivated women who have been in the exact same spot you are in right now. Women, who have taken the same classes, can give you advice on which Professors are best, and can be the shoulder you didn't know you needed. Joining a sorority made my whole college experience. I quickly met SO many women who shared the same values as I did and three years after graduation, we are still just as close. You have nothing to lose; if you hate it after the first day, you can drop out. If you join and decide it's not for you, you can drop it then, too. But it's such an amazing way to meet A LOT of people, really fast. I remained friends with people who went through recruitment and decided it wasn't for them because we had such a great time just getting to know each other.

Greek life kept me accountable for my grades, my actions, got me involved in volunteer work, joined a bible study again, and most importantly, I was able to learn and grow so much with the women around me. I had a place to call home *in this big scary place called college and a hundred women who always had my back. I am not naïve; I know that it's just not for some people. I truly would encourage everyone to just give it a chance. It seems so intimidating, but in all honesty, everyone there went through it, too and wants to help you find your home. And what's the worst that can happen? You don't like it? At least you gave it a chance, met some new people along the way, and are that much closer to finding a different niche on your campus.*

Final Round

Lastly, I want to make sure and point out that although I personally was involved in a sorority, I had plenty of friends that it just wasn't their scene. You need to know that this is 100% okay and that it is not for everyone. Please remember that your life will not be over if you don't receive the bid from your favorite sorority. There are so many other opportunities on campus, like the clubs and organizations mentioned in the next lesson that will fill your cup to the top with so many friends, activities, and memories!

LESSON #5

We Be Clubbin'

Got 99 problems, but finding a club isn't one. If there were an emoji that could accurately describe my feelings towards clubs and organizations on college campuses, it would likely be the girl emoji, pink shirt, with her hands up in the air looking a little overwhelmed. You know which one I am talking about! Now, I believe she was doing this sign in a good way when talking about college clubs and organizations because there are just SO many clubs to choose from. Ever wanted to chase squirrels around campus or discuss your mutual love for all things bagels? These are real life clubs that were formed at colleges.

Hey, you're in college now, you can form any club you want! Typically, there will be a day assigned on campus for club sign-ups, similar to a carnival fair - minus the creepy clowns. If you want to spend your weekends skiing, there's a club for that. If you want to join a wizards and muggles club for all my *Harry Potter* fanatics out there, there's a club for that. There's even a club for line dancing, go get your dance on girl! I'm pretty sure I needed a tank top that read "so many clubs, so little time." This is one of the best parts about college because no matter what type of lifestyle, hobbies, interests, or simply just wanting to try something new, you can find a club for just about anything. Dang it, I should have started the "Ketchup is Life" club when I had the chance. #regrets

Confession time, I may or may not have signed up for a little thing my friend and I liked to call, "Country Cuties." Yes, a girl from the Midwest who grew up listening to country music while driving the county back roads and another girl coming from the West Coast who had never really listened to country music decided to start their own radio show. Why you ask? Because we could! Honestly, there is no better time to step outside of your comfort zone than in college. This friend and I always had some big ideas (she is my "adventure is out there" friend) and well, this was one of them that we came up with when trying to decide how to end our senior year of college. Let me tell you, we had a blast! We probably had a total of around fifteen top listeners (thanks to our beloved grandmas, parents, pets, and siblings), but we honestly had some of the best times.

Before our weekly show, we would post pictures on Instagram to give our loyal (ha) followers a little sneak peek into our next show. We had the breakup themed edition show, the Carrie Underwood night, and who could forget the red, white, and blue God Bless America show. If you told me in high school that I would have my own radio show (I am talking legit audio equipment, speakers and all), I probably would have started laughing out loud just thinking about it. If it wasn't for the radio club, I would have never been able to chat about my Midwestern roots, give shout outs to dogs listening, or play around with cow sound effects. College clubs and organizations are there for a reason. They are there for you to have fun, pick up a new hobby, and a great way to meet some new friends with similar interests. Did I mention that we had alias names and sometimes still post photos that we will be having a reunion show on Facebook? Have to give our loyal followers what they want!

Added Bonus:

Did you know that whether you are joining a sorority or any organization on campus, you are also building up that resume of yours? Most students don't realize the impact that these clubs have on their future. Just think...your involvement in planning that campus-wide event or raising money for your upcoming fundraiser are all great tools that future recruiters are looking for in an employee. It's a win-win situation. My recent employer even asked me about my radio show and even listened to a few episodes (mildly embarrassed to this day) during my in-person interview when I was right out of college. Don't worry, I still get jokes about it to this day from them. At the end of the day, you are having a blast with friends while also benefiting your future by joining any type of organization on campus. Where do I sign up?

LESSON #6

The Art of
Keeping Your Faith

Whether your religion, your passions, or whatever your beliefs, keeping your faith is a key ingredient to your college experience. I have to say that college is a unique time in your life because you have the opportunity to connect with such a diverse group of individuals. Take full advantage. College is a time to learn about different cultures, backgrounds, and organizations. Whether you are spiritual or not, having that group of people with similar or different beliefs will allow you to grow as an individual and expand on your knowledge of the world around you.

Over time, you realize that the universe places certain people in your life for a reason. Whether to challenge you, teach you a lesson, or simply be a friend, there is always a purpose for those who enter into your life. I would have never dreamed that I would have met one of my dearest friends, who would soon become an addition at all of our family events, if it weren't for my college experience. He is from the Congo. Coming from two so diverse backgrounds, the Midwest and the Congo, we both had the opportunity to learn about each other's faith, religion, nationality, and overall ways of life. I can honestly say that he changed my family and me for the better. He taught us the value of appreciation and provided us with a broader perspective of the world around us. You never know whom you may have the privilege to encounter while in college, that is what makes college so unique. Thanks for the friendship, Wasim!

Define Faith:

According to Merriam-Webster dictionary, faith is defined as having *a strong belief or trust in someone or something*. Faith can have a religious connotation, but according to the definition, the word can be used for multiple aspects of our lives. I like to think of the word faith as a component of our life purpose. Whether you have a passion for volunteering in one's college community, serving at a local non-profit organization, or simply donating to a canned food drive, finding one's passion is vital in keeping your faith. With everything going on in today's world, a little dose of kindness can go a long way. I encourage you to find your own sense of faith in the college setting. This will provide you with more stability and purpose while in the sometimes crazy world known as college.

LESSON #7

Balancing Act:
Book Smart

We are now going to recite a pledge as follows (created by yours truly):

I, insert name, am going to enjoy my college experience to the fullest.

I vow to be social, have way too much fun, and to call my parents on a regular basis.

Among all of this, I vow to place my grades and classes at the top of my priority list...

Even when the REALLY cute guy from Statistics asks me on a date the night before our exam.

The question I hear from a lot of young women is this, how in the world did you manage it all in college? Maintaining your grades, being in a sorority, participating in athletics, volunteering, working, interning, having a boyfriend, being social? Well, unfortunately, there isn't a one-word answer to this question or I would obviously tell you. I instead picture myself carrying a full load of books, with each book representing a different section of my life; classes, projects and papers, social life, sorority, organizations, work and internships, dates, and friendships. You have to realize that at some point, you can't carry ALL of these books on your own. You almost have to sit down and sort through which books are needed and which can be saved for later. For me, I really wanted to do it all, but I knew that would come at a certain cost. I knew that my book at the top of my stack (highest priority) had to be my classes.

At the end of the day, we are all attending college for a reason…to get an education that will lead us to our careers for the rest of our lives. May sound boring and you may doze off just reading it, but we all have to agree that it is true. I had to realize that it was okay to miss that one social event or girl's night out because I knew the importance of maintaining my grades. I would have rather spent my evening gossiping about guys and eating ice cream, but there were some nights when I sadly had to say no because class deadlines were approaching (womp, womp… such a buzz kill). I then placed my book of work and internships under that quite heavy class book. I really tried to place internships where I felt fit best into my schedule. I knew better than to choose an internship during a time where I was taking one of my hardest classes.

Placing my classes as my top priority and work and internships under that provided me with a strong foundation for my life. I knew that if I felt strongly about where I was in my classes, that in turn would affect the rest of my life; relationships, overall health, and stress.

What I like to call the "fun reads," you know those books that you pick up for your weekend getaway or road trips, was the rest of my life. My sorority, social life, dates, organizations, you get the picture. These are all great things – don't get me wrong, but I knew that those came with a lot of hard work due to the highest priority books on my shelf being my classes, work, and internships. Balancing it all can be quite tricky sometimes, but I hope these tips serve you with some helpful insight.

Be able to prioritize.

There will be times that you have to place studying above the big party. Trust me, you won't regret it when you get back your test scores on Monday. I know in high school it was somewhat acceptable to cram for your exam that morning, but procrastination is not going to fly in college. You may think that you can keep up with that lifestyle, but it will sadly only do you harm. Take time to prioritize your checklist for the day, placing your schoolwork above anything else.

Attend Professor office hours.

This one-on-one time may seem daunting at first, but I promise you that they will appreciate you making the effort to get a better understanding of the class material. If nothing else, you will stand out to them and they will remember you. Still deciding if that's a good or bad thing...kidding.

Learn to balance.

College isn't all tests and papers and projects, even though it may seem like this at times. The feeling when you receive an "A" on that paper that you have been working your tail off for...this deserves some celebration. Be able to mix some fun in there when you can! You deserve it! If you have already met with your Professor and feel as though a certain class is not the right fit for you or you have room in your schedule to add another class, please be aware when the drop/add week is for your college. This is a week where students are allowed to drop or add a class without penalty. Please keep in mind to try and stay in any freshman level course if at all possible to keep you on track to graduate on time. Imagine, you just finished your last final of your freshman year, what are you going to do next? I'm going to Disney World!!! Hey, a girl can dream, right?

Acquire a study buddy.

Always try and find a study buddy in your classes. Your buddy will hold you accountable, be there to answer any questions that you may have from class, and share some laughs with you at your 2 a.m. library visit when you are dancing to weird music videos just to keep yourselves awake and watching cat fail videos on repeat. You laugh now, but this *will* happen to you. During finals week, be ready to give up your *Netflix* and social media passwords to your trusted study buddy to change for the week. The only codes you will be needing is the code to the library after hours.

Navigate your life with your planner.

I recommend purchasing a planner because that was one item I couldn't live without in college. Place EVERYTHING in here, deadlines for papers and projects, social events, date nights, weekend trips, etc. It will soon become your best friend that may also cause you to have a mental breakdown if you ever lose it.

Create your study space.

Carve out time in your schedule each week for dedicated library time. Book a room at your library or find that one study spot you can call your home for the next year(s). I don't recommend using your dorm or apartment. You will easily get distracted by your roomies, music, tempting nap situations, and outside noise. Not that the sometimes VERY comfy library chairs are just asking for you to take a nap in them, but maybe you will steer away since you're out in public and don't want to get caught drooling by the cute guy from Statistics. Yes, libraries are there for a reason (shocking - I know), so study on my friend!

Engage in the classroom.

Whether by taking thoughtful notes, speaking up in class, or simply keeping up on the weekly readings, the last thing that you want to do is fall behind. Learn to love your classes (even the dreadful ones) because you don't want to have to take them again. Let's avoid that to keep you sane! Here is my go-to advice for classroom tips to productively engage in the classroom; sit in the first or second row (sitting in the back causes distractions of all kinds), try and take handwritten notes and avoid using your computer during class (you may get a hand cramp but it's better than spending class online shopping/Facebook creeping), join or create a Facebook group for your class (perfect for comparing class notes and finding study groups), and learn to love presentations (they happen more than you would like in college, so be ready to embrace your public speaking skills). *Freshman Tip* - Ever heard of the unspoken fifteen-minute rule? Start a countdown on your phone if your Professor is MIA. The fifteen-minute rule is when your Professor does not show up for class after fifteen minutes, then you are technically free to leave. It is comparable to winning the college lottery. Enjoy!

Need a laugh after all this book talk? A friend of mine once took off her sweatshirt only to find out that she only had a sports bra on in front of 70 people in the very front of her lecture hall. You live and you learn, right?

Book Smart Fun Facts:

Speaking of books, I wanted to touch base on the topic of purchasing textbooks. This lovely addition to your budget can quite quickly add up. You want to save some money for your late night food runs, right? Well, a quick tip is to do your research on your assigned textbooks. There are now websites available where you can rent your textbooks for SO much cheaper (sorry, college bookstores). You can just rent the textbook for a certain semester and then send it back to the company after your finals. I highly recommend using the website, Chegg, for all your book rental needs. The only thing that will be "lit" will be your wallet because it will be on fire with all that extra cash. Bad analogy, I promise I'm cooler in person. You may even have extra money to get yourself that late night slice of pizza! Did someone say pizza? I'm in!

LESSON #8

Case of the Homesick Blues

What do you mean that I won't get to see my parents until Homecoming weekend? It seems like all of my old high school friends are adjusting and loving college life? Am I the only one feeling this case of homesickness?

I promise you that even your high school best friend who is continuously posting photos of how much she is LOVING college has had the same feelings as you at one point or another. The feeling of homesickness is completely, 100% normal. I still catch myself being homesick, even as a twenty-five year old. I should probably work on that. There is something about the start of college where you can't help but feel sad missing your home, parents, siblings, or even your dog, Wrigley. Whether you moved two hours away or are states away from home, the transition can still be difficult, yet manageable with the right attitude. The best part about it though is the nostalgic feeling you get when you do go home and how much you start to appreciate the little things.

The truth is that in the next few months, you will have two "homes." Your forever home will always be your go-to place of comfort, but your second home will soon become the community that you create for yourself at college. Trust me from experience, there will come a time where you will feel as though you have created another home for yourself, where you are eager to get back to campus after the holidays. No offense Mom and Dad! You will be ready to get back to your new friends, social life, events, and hey, maybe even classes? Say it isn't so!

The icing on the cake is that you know in your heart that you will always have your family, siblings, pets, and hometown to turn to in times of need during your journey. It took me quite a while to have that home feeling... about a full year. It was not until I made up my mind that my final college would be where I would call home before I started to feel at peace. There were definitely difficult days where I wished I could just click my heels together three times and be back in the comforts of home, but I knew it was going to take some effort on my end. Clicking my Converses together would sadly still return me to my dorm room, but now I have to endure strange looks from my roommate, great. It took time and I worked hard to step outside of my comfort zone, joined campus organizations, and I finally found the set of friends who would make me laugh when I was crying about a guy, took me to get froyo when I was stressing about finals, and most importantly, made sure that I was having fun. May sound corny, but it honestly made me forget about the feelings of homesickness and instead made me realize how fortunate I was to be in a place I could also call home. Contrary to popular beliefs, I am a firm advocate that good things are going to happen to you. Just may take some extra courage and confidence in yourself.

A common theme during the first semester of your freshman year is the ever-popular road trips to visit your friends at other colleges. Some of your high school friends may even all attend the same college, which can cause feelings of FOMO and hurt feelings. I love the idea of spending some time seeing your bestie from high school and experiencing his or her world of new friends and a new environment, but I want to highly encourage you to hold off until your second semester for these visits. You need time to focus on YOUR new life and establishing YOUR foundation at YOUR college. Visiting friends at other colleges can sometimes lead to having feelings of jealousy and may even lead to second guessing yourself on your decision to attend your college. Take time to build your foundation and use time during the holidays to preserve those high school friendships!

Lastly, please keep in mind that you never truly know what other people could be going through in life. Whether on your dorm floor, a classmate, or a stranger in passing, my hope is that you show kindness and be the friend that they might need during this crazy thing called college. I believe that every person has his or her own story and it may just take a special person to reach out and listen. Just think, if each one of you seek out a classmate or peer who you see may be struggling, can you imagine how many friendships would be made? One less person who feels lonely and isolated on campus. My wish is that you be that friend to someone your freshman year.

Another way to connect with not only your peers, but with your college community, is by volunteering your time to help tutor kids at a local school in your area. Many schools have after school programs that would love the mentorship of college students. My college offered a similar program and the college mentors would always end the semester by saying that they hoped to have inspired the kids, but the kids in turn inspired them. By reaching out a hand to the next generation of youth, you will become a role model and support system to those children in need.

For those of you who are enjoying the college life a little too much and may tend to forget to call your parents, do me a favor and give them a call. They, too, may be feeling homesick from missing you!

Take it from a dear friend of mine who has been in this "homesick blues" state of mind. With a little time and campus engagement, Ellen quickly found the cure to her blues. Let's find out how.

Everyone told me that college would be the best four years of my life, so naturally, I expected to show up and everything would just fall into place! I felt so discouraged as I found myself in my dorm room, crying on the phone with my parents for what felt like the first month I was there. I was lucky enough to have a very close knit group of friends in high school and I was nervous about leaving them all, as I was one of the only ones who chose a school not knowing a single person. My parents told me it would be great to break away from the people I had known my whole life and gain a whole new group of friends. But as all my other friends from home were joining the same sorority and fraternities together, I found myself doubting my decision. I was overwhelmed and felt so alone.

The first week of school there were tons of activity fairs and floor activities to get to know the other girls on my dorm floor. At the beginning though, I felt like I was just going through the motions. I was joining activities and meeting new people, but I wasn't really "trying." I wasn't truly giving that place and those people a real chance. I missed my parents, I called them multiple times every day. I missed my dogs. I didn't like the food. I missed my friends...the list could go on and on. And worst of all, my parents wouldn't let me have a car on campus. My Dad said, "It would ruin my freshman year experience." Like most times in life, my parents were right.

After about a month, I finally got the hang of how classes worked and how to organize myself. I started to figure out the halls that had better food and on which days. I started to actually engage with the people I had met and realized they were pretty great. And before I knew it, I found myself calling my parents only once a day, and then every other day. Don't get me wrong, even as a *senior after a bad day there is nothing I wanted more than to be cuddling with my puppies eating a home cooked meal, but I began to not only make it work but actually began to enjoy myself. I started to realize that every other person I was meeting was in the exact same position as me. We were all starting this whole new journey and frankly, not any of us knew what we were doing.*

I began to lean on my new friends, the friends that were experiencing the exact same struggles during their transition. On difficult days, I didn't have my parents to hug, but I did have a dorm full of girls eating Oreos and watching chick flicks, and that started to seem pretty darn great. You are going to get homesick, it's natural. College is scary, overwhelming, and challenging. But not having my car forced me to be a "college kid." I couldn't go home every weekend, so I started to hang out with friends all weekend and found myself having a BLAST. I couldn't just get in my car and drive somewhere when I didn't like the food. Instead, my roommate and I would walk somewhere to-gether off campus and get to know each other even more. There is a reason everyone says that college is the best four years of your life. So take a second, try to embrace the change, and find yourself. Trust yourself. Your support system is always a call away, but you will miss out on so much if you just focus on all of the things that are no longer the same.

If you didn't get a picture or document it on social media, did it even happen? In today's generation, social media is beginning to take over our thoughts, ideas, and emotions. We are constantly comparing our lives to those that we may know absolutely nothing about, which sadly can lead to feelings of jealousy and loneliness. Take it from a dear friend of mine, Marnie, on her advice for combatting loneliness, in a world of so-called perfect Instagram photos and perceptions.

As much as it seems like it, no one really has their life in order. Everyone wants to be perceived as effortlessly smart, successful, kind, hilarious, and beautiful. We broadcast idealized snippets of our lives – Instagramming that picture where our hair looks amazing or we did something cool.

Agonizing over a caption that strikes the right tone — both funny and heartwarming, cool and smart, witty and uncomplicated. We Snapchat pictures of our friends and our pets and our most exciting adventures, but these snippets of our lives are only half the story.

We don't Snapchat the hours we spend struggling to study for a test, the times we sit alone in our rooms, argue with our friends, or don't feel fabulous. We don't Instagram our acne or love handles or bad hair days. So what are we greeted with on social media? Glossy, idealized versions of everyone we know. We see their best moments, not their everyday ones. This can make it very easy to feel alone. To feel like the boring, ugly duckling on the sideline of everyone else's fabulous, fast-paced lives. The thing is, everyone feels this way.

You are not alone, and no one is living a fabulous, fast-paced life all the time. We all have times when we sit in our beds wearing that one ratty t-shirt and binge watching TV shows, even though we have a million things to do. We all have times when we feel homesick and friendsick and lovesick. We all have times when we feel like we can't do anything right. But that is what makes our lives so full. The good times wouldn't be nearly as sweet without the tough ones.

The best way that I've found to combat feeling alone in these down times is to be vulnerable. It is the hardest thing to do until you make it a practice in your life. Being vulnerable means showing your true self to others. It means being willing to tell someone when you've had a bad day, feel unprepared for a test, or are feeling homesick. It also means being willing to share what you love. It is being willing to tell someone your biggest dreams, the places you want to travel, your greatest hopes. It means cutting through that glossy façade we all put forward to instead be the real, authentic person underneath.

Being vulnerable about your true self instantly sets others at ease and allows them to open up as well. It is amazing how quickly others will rush to share their feelings when you share yours. Sharing feelings and wishes and true selves takes vulnerability, but it's amazing how quickly it brings intimacy and solidarity and joy and fullness to your relationships.

Be vulnerable. Get to know your true self and share that person with others. You will find such joy and fullness in the process.

Dear Diary:

As Ralph Waldo Emerson eloquently stated, "self-trust is the first secret of success." Ladies, please know your limits and if the pressure gets to be too much, I want you to know that there is always free counseling offered on campus. Whether body image, overwhelming classes, homesickness, stress, or you may simply just need someone to talk to, it is not seen as a weakness but only as a strength in my eyes. Your RA (Resident Assistant) *refer back to lesson 1* is also a great resource in times of need. Just remember, someone who values themselves enough to seek help when needed is a sign of one strong individual! Keeping your mental health strong is a key ingredient to your overall well-being. You ladies already inspire me!

LESSON #9

Swipe Right
College Dating 101

Bumble, Tinder, Pizza Love Match, wait…I wish there was an app for that! In this crazy world of dating, having a guy ask a girl out for a date IN PERSON is almost unheard of. There is still something unique about having real conversations in person. Yes, it may be scary, but I believe in you. There is life out there outside of your mobile device. That, I promise you! Simply put, dating in today's world can be…awkward. Very, very awkward. The thing is, you have to realize that you're not alone in this process. You also need to understand that unfortunately boys are still boys. I wish there was fairy dust that could magically change them from the high school boy to the mature college guy, but sadly that transition does not happen over a quick summer break. Sometimes, you just have to laugh when your date sends you a Venmo request after your dinner date for your meal. Other times, you just have to learn to not take dating so seriously. One day he's acting like Romeo and the next day, poof, he's gone! I believe that if a guy "ghosts" you, then he wasn't worth your time in the first place. You deserve better than an odd ghost haunting you anyway. Not sure that's how it works, but let's go with it. The only thing I want to be doing while watching *Netflix* involves – *Netflix* and Chick-fil-A. *Side Dish* - One of the worst things you can do to yourself is crave Chick-fil-A, drive to your nearest Chick-fil-A, only to find out it's…*Sunday*. Cue the tears now.

As Princess Diana states, "People think that at the end of the day a man is the only answer. Actually, a fulfilling job is better for me." They always say, you have to kiss a lot of frogs to find your prince, right? Well, let's just say these failed dating stories left the frogs abandoned on their own lily pads. I omitted the names to protect the innocent, please enjoy.

The date ended and I really didn't want it to end with the classic goodnight kiss, so when he leaned in, I instead went for a high-five (I had no other genius idea). Worst part, he wasn't ready for it, so he missed the high-five and I just ran inside as fast as I could.

I had braces beginning my freshman year and was asked out on a date to the movie theaters. We got to the movies a little later than we expected and ended up in the front row. While he turned to sort the popcorn into separate containers, I sneezed and pressed my face into my favorite new scarf to avoid being shushed by the mass of teenage girls behind us. In doing so, my braces got stuck to the threads of my scarf and would not unhook. I turned away from my date mortified that he would see this mishap. I tugged so incredibly hard on my scarf that the brackets on a few of my front teeth popped off and released the threads.

Miraculously, he didn't notice my Hulk-like tug, but he did ask if the popcorn had broken some of my brackets when we left the parking garage. Not only did I ruin my scarf, but I also had to go to the orthodontist the next day to fix the broken brackets. Long story short, my teeth were sore for the next couple of days and he ended the night with a kiss on the cheek. However, we did end up dating for a year and a half afterwards, braces and all!

I was home on holiday break and my older brother and his best friend crashed my first date. We were at the movies and I heard noises behind us and turned around to see the two of them sitting in the movie theater with beanies and sunglasses on "chaperoning." That guy got rid of me faster than you can say, "can you pass the popcorn?"

Time for a funny story from a guy's perspective. So this girl texts me (she's a friend) and asks to get some coffee. I say sure, thinking it'll be a friendly get coffee and chat type of thing. She gets there first and as I show up I look through the window and see her staring out at me and then quickly glance back down. Weird. I go in, "hey, what's up, how are you," the usual. The host comes over and asks if we are ready. I say I just got here and need a minute to decide. So, he says I'll bring out some water. Conversation starts normal, lots of small talk. Waiter arrives and he says he will be back in a minute. The conversation slows to a dramatic lull. Small talk becomes extreme small talk. Silence. We just keep sipping our water and no one has come to take our order. That's when I realized that this is a date. I'm on a date and WE ONLY HAVE WATER. Thirty-five minutes later someone FINALLY comes to take our order and she orders a LARGE CAPPUCCINO. Small talk is not even close to what's happening anymore, it's more just staring at walls and occasionally saying, "it's cold" or something. The check FINALLY comes and her eyes glance up at me to pay the check. Long story short, we never spoke again.

Tinder picture looked like Ryan Gosling (score). Real life looked like Russell Brand (he even had a better man bun than me).

On my first date, he asked during dinner if he could kiss my ear???

My brother and this girl met for the first time upon arriving at the restaurant. There were awkward hellos exchanged at the door and then they were seated. My brother asked if they had soup because he had mouth surgery a few days prior and chewing food was still a little rough. They didn't have soup, so it was explained that the "softest" food on the menu was gnocchi. He ordered the house gnocchi and proceeded to cut each tiny dumpling into four or more pieces and slowly chew each piece. He ate the entire dish over a three-hour period and the girl stuck it out the entire time. Three. Whole. Hours. I'm pretty sure they never saw each other again.

He told me he went to jail on our first date. End of story.

When you've been messaging back and forth in hopes of a first date and go to Facebook to creep on his page and it says "in a relationship."

I never made it past the token "Yogurtland" date in college.

Dating Tip: Good luck. You're welcome.

Looking back now, I realized that I learned some valuable life lessons from relationships while in college. I absolutely enjoyed going on dates, formal outings, and walking the quaint circle at nights. I wouldn't have traded those memories for the world. If you so happen to meet your college match one day like a T-Swift song in a coffee shop, my only advice would be to make sure that you continue to maintain your relationships with your roommates, friends, and classmates. I felt as though I tried hard to not always choose my "bae" over my friends, but looking back, I kind of wish that I had made more of an effort in that department. I just so happened to meet a great guy who I enjoyed spending my days with roaming around campus, but that does not mean that you have to sacrifice friendships. Keeping your schoolwork, friends, and personal time at the top of your priority list is strongly recommended. Being your strong, independent self is key, prior to meeting a cute guy in your class. Please also keep in mind that going on a date or two won't hurt ya! You never know, your "swipe right" may be sitting in the coffee shop at the table next to you. Take note!

Still crushing on your high school sweetheart? Are you both attending the same or different colleges? The only reason that I ask is because either way, it will change your freshman experience. I highly advise that you take some time the summer before you begin college and discuss the transition and some potential obstacles. I'm sure it can be amazing and comforting having your boyfriend by your side throughout your crazy first semester, but it can also be jeopardizing to your experience. Please keep in mind these tips: If he is attending a different college from you, try and plan some weekends at your separate colleges. If your boyfriend visits you every weekend or vice versa, this will limit each of you from meeting new friends and experiencing the freshman lifestyle. Being jealous of the other attending parties or events without you is simply going to happen. Beware of the "turkey dump"…I'll let you look that one up for yourself. Also, if you are attending the same college, I advise you to still remain independent individuals. Try and join separate organizations and create your own identity and friend group on campus. All that said, high school and long distance relationships are doable, just know your boundaries!

Always remember to trust your friends and family in these situations. I know that their advice may not be what you want to hear at the time, but just remember they are the ones that know you best. If you break up with your college sweetheart, just remember, there is a reason why it is called a breakup...because it was broken. In some shape or form, you were not meant to be and one day you will look back and know the reason why. Until then, trust the ones that love you most and know that you will be just fine on your own. *Relationship Thoughts* - I am always wondering what my type in guys really is? I want to find someone that is supportive and fun to be around, active, and is there for me on both my good and bad days. Dang it...I'm just describing my yoga pants again.

Don't get me wrong, I am a huge fan of gathering with girlfriends every Monday night to watch a reality TV show in our sweatpants, with full on corkboards of our favorite contestants, and in our "We're Getting Pizza After This" tank tops. *Side Note* - watch for the contestants with the popular "I Woke Up Like This" shirts on and please take note. LIES. Come on, I guarantee you that the contestant whose makeup "happens to look perfect from the night before" and hair could be ready to be photographed for *Vogue* are all lies. The reality is that when I wake up in the morning, I look pretty similar to Anna on *Frozen* when she finds out that it is coronation day, but add on some zit cream. I should just let it go, I guess. Jokes for days.

My point is that yes, these reality television shows can be a fun social gathering, but it is also a huge reality check for real life dating. Do I wish my first date with the cute guy from Statistics could magically say instead of going to Baskin-Robbins for ice cream, we are instead getting on this private helicopter to a private island to make our own ice cream from scratch? Well, of course. The truth is that the word, reality, does not necessarily correlate to reality in the dating world. I feel like I'm considered "lucky" if he just offers to buy my ice cream. Don't worry, I am sure it was for the "right reasons." Also, you may want to run now if he weirdly asks you to accept a rose at the end of the date! Just a suggestion.

To all my single ladies out there! I want you to know that being single in college is also one of the best decisions that you can make. These are your only years to do the things that YOU want to do, be independent, and take time to grow as an individual. You go, girl (insert applause). Lastly, I want to say a thank you to all the couples out there that welcome us single ladies as third wheels. We appreciate the extra meals, additional dance partners, and letting us photobomb your adorable "candid laughing" Insta photos. If for some reason Blake Lively and Ryan Reynolds are reading this, I am a great third wheel. Maybe they could introduce me to Zac Efron? Don't worry, I'll send you all a save the date to our "High School Musical" themed wedding, cheesy choreography included.

Caution Flag!

Let's try and avoid those overserved college guys at parties. Not always good news, no matter how old or cool they say they are! Trust me, especially the seniors. You will thank me later for this one!

LESSON #10

Red Solo Cup – Honesty Hour

First things first, I want you to know that all college parties are not like the ones that you have seen in the movies or on your favorite television show. I'm not saying that you can't find those types of parties in the college world (#honestyhour), but I am confident that you know yourself well enough to sort out the type of party that is right for you. I want to be up-front with you because I am pretty sure we have already become best friends back in lesson #5? At least I hope so! I am not the girl that is labeled as a "party starter" and I am not the girl who does not remember what happened the night before. Honestly, that is just not me and it has taken some time for me to learn this over the years. I am the girl who has attended the so-called crazy fraternity formals, date parties, tailgates, and 21st birthday bashes, but through it all, I remained the "Emily" that I was proud to be the next morning. There were no "walk of shame" regrets in my book. Now, I have to admit that my all-time favorite "night out on the town" had to be my girl's night in spent watching sappy chick flicks, rehashing failed weekend dates, all while in sweats eating ice cream and Snapchatting our "epic" night. I personally would rather spend my Friday nights not being stepped all over and spilled on at a club, but hey that's just me.

One of my all-time favorite words of advice from my Mom before I left for college was this: Just because you are holding a red solo cup, doesn't mean that there has to be alcohol in it. She would tell me all the time that when she was in college, she would go to all of the fun college parties, but she would bring a Diet Coke and fill her red solo cup up and no one ever knew. Can you say GENIUS? Think about it, in this day and age, a red solo cup signifies that you are "drinking," so if you feel uncomfortable, remember this trick. I know it seems crazy but you can still have fun at a party without the excessive drinking. I learned this from one very wise woman. Not trying to be your Mom here, but this was a topic that I was very concerned about when going into college, so I want to make sure that I am being transparent with you ladies.

Peer pressure, especially around drinking and recreational drugs, is out there. It was around when our parents were in college and sadly still is today. Just know that you are in control of *your* own actions and hold only *yourself* accountable. Finding the right group of friends is key in this situation. Just because one group of friends may pressure you to do something, doesn't mean that you will never find another group of friends who aren't into that scene. I will never forget one of my first weekends at the first college I attended. It was not only a very large party school, but it was also a rated party school. I didn't realize this until I experienced my first weekend there. You live and you learn, right? The girls were *expected* to only wear skirts or dresses when going out, I quickly learned what a "pregame" was, and it didn't take long for me to see that I didn't fit in there. There were definitely moments where I just wanted to fit in and could see myself going down a different path. Doesn't everyone have those moments where they want to be a part of that certain popular group or just feel like you belong?

Fast forward to my last college, I remember laughing at the thought of us HAVING to wear skirts or dresses if we wanted to go out because my friends and I went out to a party in our sweats and t-shirts, because we honestly just didn't feel like dressing up. We still laugh about it to this day! It wasn't until I made it to my final college until I realized how proud I was of myself for putting my foot down at the first college and realizing that not all college experiences had to be like that. Yes, my friends and I would still go out, attended fun fraternity and sorority formals, and danced until our feet hurt. The key was that I surrounded myself with friends who knew me for me. They knew my funny traits, my limits, and never did I feel pressured by them. It may take some time, but I have full confidence in you that you will one day find your group of friends that know you well enough that you feel comfortable in any setting with them.

By surrounding yourself with positive people, you are setting yourself up for success in several aspects of your life. *Throwback Thursday* - Hey, this works really well because it was actually on a Thursday. Winning at life. Anyways, I'll never forget when I went out to my friend's 21st birthday after a workout wearing my leggings and sweatshirt while sipping on my dollar Diet Coke and holding her birthday gift of a balloon dog on a stick (you know those inflatable dogs you can purchase and walk around the mall). Some of my best memories happened with the friends that knew me the best and I'm forever grateful for them.

Oh yea, and did I mention? You will have the time of your life with them! Dance until you can't dance anymore and maybe invest in a balloon dog that you can walk around at parties (great conversation starter). When you get older, there are sometimes even real dogs at parties (score, you don't have to even socialize with real people), one of the few perks of getting older and having your own place. "Adulting" as they call it these days, that's for another book.

Foodie Alert - Brunch is becoming America's favorite pastime for a reason. Put on your trendy sunnies, a cute choker with your floral dress, add your floppy hat and you're ready for the brunch scene. Can you say delicious french toast all while in an adorable setting with close friends? If going out isn't your cup of tea (pun intended), brunch is the perfect option to meet up with friends but not be out until sunrise. *Do Not Disturb* - you also get to experience this thing called sleep. Yes, this little thing called sleep does wonders for you and is a must while in college. I'm a big fan of brunch for those reasons, now can you pass the syrup please?

PSA

I know this sounds cliché but I 100% ask you to take this section seriously. Please don't drink and drive under ANY circumstance. Watch your drink at all times and always remain with a buddy. These may seem like small things at the time, but I beg of you to drink responsibly once you are of legal age. It is critical that you are always aware of your surroundings and are keeping a watchful eye on your drinks. Please remember that once you leave your red solo cup, *that cup is no longer yours*. The minute you step away from your drink, you can no longer trust what someone has possibly placed in your cup after you walked away. Lastly, please never let your friends go anywhere at night by themselves. USE THE BUDDY SYSTEM. Unfortunately, I lost a dear friend from a similar situation where a buddy was needed. I know this sounds silly or like you are at summer camp, but pick out your buddy before you leave for the night and be responsible for one another.

Safety on college campuses is their number one priority. Whether walking home from a night class, leaving a workout late at night, or simply feeling unsafe, please call your campus safe ride number. These are designated safety officers whose sole purpose is to keep students safe. They are hired for a reason, use them. They will provide this information at orientation. Save the number in your phone and know that there will always be a safe option home. Lastly, I want you to know that although drinking can make you feel invincible at times, it does not mean that you have free rein to do anything. I am not here to tell you what you can or cannot do, but I am here to let you know that there are consequences to your actions, which can severely affect the rest of your college experience. I beg of you to please drink responsibly and be in control of your own actions. I thank you in advance for listening!

LESSON #11

Freshman Fifteen
Kicked to the Curb

You know when you've really made it is when you get to order ANYTHING you want and have ANYTHING you want twenty-four hours a day. This, my friends is called college living. It is kind of like living on a cruise ship, without the beach, beautiful sunsets, pool, well…maybe not exactly. Cruise ships offer food anytime you are hungry, similar to college. Now, throughout your college experience, you will go from Mom's home cooked meals, to the dorm cafeteria, to one day living on your own to fend for yourself = the worst. My piece of advice is to get a meal plan for at least your freshman and sophomore year. It may not seem "cool" at the time, but trust me, the only thing uncool will be you trying to make your own meals in your small community kitchen with virtually no pots and pans. Your only meal prep will consist of packing your leftover last night pizza slices for the entire week. I do recommend buying some snacks and a few frozen meals to store in your dorm mini fridge just in case you don't have time to run to your cafeteria or the weather turns on you. Trust me, we all know that you don't want to mess with a hangry girl who has basically no food left in her fridge.

So, a meal plan is also a great way to connect and make new friends. The cafeteria or otherwise known as "the caf" at my college, turned into a social outing because it was where I met the majority of my friends. Now, I have to admit that it depends on each college campus, but the food is not the same as your momma's cooking. Beware of the mystery meat. If you cannot identify the color or content of the food item, it is better off to pass on it. I just thought I should warn you now. They do offer a variety of meals, but I wouldn't set your expectations too high. This will make you grateful for your home cooked meals when you return home for the holidays! I can smell the turkey cooking now in the kitchen.

Along with the unlimited amount of food options and quantities comes the dreaded "freshman fifteen." For those of you unaware of this term, it is typically said that most freshmen gain around fifteen pounds during their freshman year alone. I mean who wouldn't want late night free pizza or hotdogs? There are times when you can't resist that kind of deal. Am I right? Personally, I believe that you can fight off the dreaded "freshman fifteen" with a few simple tips. On your way to the ice cream machine, also make sure to locate the salad bar station. Yes, the cafeteria does offer healthy options. No, it may not sound as appetizing as the chicken finger basket, but maybe try and wait to splurge until the weekend. Don't feel the need to try ALL the food stations in the first semester…or the first week. The food will still be there. That is something I can promise you. Now, with about every food option at your disposal, you will need to find the right combination of letting yourself splurge and maintaining a healthy diet. Indulge in the occasional late night pizza run, but balance that out with some physical activity.

Speaking of hitting the gym, I highly recommend finding a workout buddy. Most college campuses offer free workout classes during the week. Hey, you can actually workout in that athleisure you always wear to class. Try out some classes with a friend and decide on a class or two a week to attend together. It is a great way to keep each other accountable and also helps keep you Spring Break ready all year round! If the campus isn't your scene for working out, be sure to check out some local gyms and studios. A majority of them will offer some type of student discount. Finding a local trail or hike nearby is also a cost effective and fun way to explore your new college town. Make sure to use the buddy system on all hikes.

Secondly, if a workout class surrounded by sweaty people who need showers isn't your style, maybe join a club team that you find interesting that incorporates a calorie burning activity. At my college, they offered dodgeball, kickball, intermural soccer, snowboarding, tennis, and lots of other activities to keep you moving. Just because you didn't join an official athletic team doesn't mean you still can't be active. I signed up for tennis class my sophomore year of college and had the time of my life (just don't ask me how I ranked in class). I met new friends and knew that twice a week, I would be outside enjoying the spring weather while getting my workout on. I may have even improved my tennis skills, who knows!

Lastly, know that whatever size college you attend, you will be doing a lot of walking whether you like it or not. If you do not enjoy walking now, I would recommend you start liking it. Especially since most freshmen and sophomores don't typically have their cars on campus, walking becomes your best friend. *Weather Alert* - Be sure to invest in a nice rain and winter coat for the sometimes treacherous walks to and from campus. So grab your tracking device and get moving! If I sprint to the cafeteria (or more like fast walk), does that count as my cardio for the day? Asking for a friend…

Friendly Reminder

Strawberry ice cream does not count as your daily fruit intake. Nice try though!

LESSON #12

The Gift You Give
Yourself – Me Time

Let's be honest, college can be overwhelming. Just look at all of these lessons you have already read regarding a variety of different topics. Yes, college is the time of your life to "live it up" and be carefree before you enter the "real world" but an unspoken truth about college is that there are going to be times when you just want to burst into tears because you are so stressed about your upcoming midterm and there will be times when you start to feel guilty dedicating your free time to your schoolwork instead of going out with your friends. Sometimes you may just need to lay on the floor and cry because #life (seems dramatic but necessary at times and weirdly makes you feel better). The one piece of advice that stuck out to me throughout my years in college was to be sure to set aside "me" time.

When I say "me" time I don't mean sitting with your roommate binge watching *Netflix* or giving yourself one minute to take a deep breath. I mean literally setting aside at least two hours a week (come on, that's not asking a lot) for uninterrupted, stress free "me" time. Nowadays, you almost feel guilty, wait, let's be honest, you do feel guilty if you have some time where you don't have any meetings to go to, class, or a social activity planned. You almost experience FOMO just sitting by yourself. To be transparent, I totally understand. I was the one in college, and still to this day, who hated being left alone and felt strangely weird if I had free time on my schedule. It all changed for me when I started my junior year attending a class called, *Self and Identity*.

This class was dedicated to personal growth, finding oneself, and it was one of the most impactful classes that I have ever attended. We did exercises dedicated to bettering oneself. My Professor challenged us one day to take two hours a week for "me" time. No phone calls, texts, scrolling through Instagram posts or sending weird selfies on Snapchat. Was it hard at first? Of course! I felt like my fingers didn't know what to do if I wasn't double tapping a photo or scrolling through screens. So, I found a tree and bought a journal and began my journey to find my "me" time.

My friends on campus began to have memorized when I would be at my tree. Every Tuesday and Thursday, I began to look forward to my tree outings. I could actually focus on my thoughts racing through my head, take in the beautiful scenery of my campus, and sometimes just people watch for the fun of it. I would create fake scenarios in my mind of what people were talking to each other about or who should date whom as I watched in our common area. Okay, now I'm just sounding weird and creepy. Whether you are practicing yoga in your happy place, finding a swing that you call your own, or writing in your journal under a tree, I challenge you to find your "me" place on campus.

You know that friend that you have to scroll down her page to make sure that you haven't missed any of her inspirational quotes or passages on Instagram? For me, I met this friend while sitting in the class mentioned above. Her words continue to speak to me and I hope they do to you, too. Get ready, she brings out all the feels. Love ya, Brittnei!

You have a choice in every matter you encounter. Whether it is who or what you give your time to, how much you study, who you surround yourself with, or what class you take each semester. There are going to be people who offer you advice – close friends, family members, student advisors – but what matters in the end is how your soul feels. Take the valuable advice, store it into your minds, and then sift it through your goals, your journey, and your ultimate dreams to see if it matches up.

Often we make choosing so much more complicated than it has to be. Something I hope that you learn and revel in is that you don't always have to follow the generally accepted rules of society. Doing that will take you far, but is it in the direction you want to be going?

Take a moment with each and every decision you are faced with and ask yourself – Will this make me happy? Does this take me closer to where

I want to be? Am I doing this for myself or someone else? And then make your decision based on your response to those questions. Of course, there are going to be decisions we have to make that we may not like (such as enrolling in Calculus), but I am referring to those outward decisions related to friendships, parties you attend, the major you choose, and the way you interact with others.

Don't be afraid to choose – and to choose differently. Trust your gut. Don't be swayed and keep pushing even when you face challenges that make you question your decisions. In the end, college is only four years. You have so many more years ahead to learn about yourself and plenty of time to do so. Also, realize the power of your words. Speak life into your situation, positivity, and actively choose how to feel.

No one can make you feel a certain way. You choose to feel certain emotions based on how you perceive the action of others. This may sound hard to understand at first, but take a moment and actively choose how you are going to feel the next time you encounter a sticky situation. Take control of your feelings, of your words, and be proud of the choices you make.

Choosing how to follow your own path will be the best decision you will ever make, I promise.

In Memory

My Professor, Doc, sadly passed away within a few months after I graduated college. He may not know it, but I kept all of his handouts, my journals, and notes from his class. He was teaching what I call my "life class" when none of us knew that he himself was dealing with one of life's biggest battles, cancer. This lesson is dedicated to you, Doc. Thank you for teaching your students what it meant to truly live and breathe a healthy and positive life. Life is too short not to!

LESSON #13

Run the World (Girls)

Just picture yourself jamming out to the Queen Beyoncé's hit song, "Run the World (Girls)" within minutes of leaving your house on your way to your newfound freedom… college. I'm talking all out, full dance moves while waiting at the stoplight, no cares in the world sing-along. Say goodbye to strict curfews, household chores, structured meals, and those monotonous 7 a.m.- 3 p.m. schedules. Say hello to budgeting your own money, learning time management, paying student loans, and juggling college bills. I'm pretty sure when Beyoncé was informing us to "get in formation," she really meant she wanted us to "get our bills in formation." Also, when she said, "slay," she really meant, "pay." Real life, am I right? Yikes, this has me wanting to crawl back home to Mom and Dad! Send help!

Yes, this "newfound freedom" may sound exhilarating at first but it only takes a few short days on campus to realize that you are REALLY on your own now. No parents to lend you money whenever you need it, no more home cooked meals at a certain time every night, and sadly no one to make sure that you have completed your homework before you begin binge watching your new favorite *Netflix* series. Now, you may be rethinking this whole living on your own thing, but I will help guide you through those first couple of months, don't you worry.

Let's begin with probably the last thing you want to hear about, budgeting. I know this sounds super lame, but it is actually very important during your first few weeks. Whether you are having to pay for college on your own or are having help from your parents, you will need to start tracking your spending no matter what situation you are in. What's a quick way to get started? Download a budget-tracking app on your phone. There are numerous ones to choose from and are simple to use, which is key! You just type in your amount spent after each purchase and select a different category type for your allowance each month. Once you go over your spending allowance for each category for the month, you will be sent an alert to let you know. Pretty easy, right? This allows you to budget for that fun college t-shirt you saw at Freshman Orientation, but will remind you that you can't purchase the whole bookstore. This will also prompt you to maybe re-think your expensive ticket to Coachella and be a news flash, reminding you that you can only afford to buy yourself an umbrella instead. Ouch, at least you will stay dry though, right? Not helping?

The must-have item to make sure you include in your budget before you head off to college is a durable laptop. Along with your planner, this item will also be your best friend, so make sure you invest your summer earnings on selecting the right one for your major. Be also on the lookout for college fare saver apps. Several colleges have an app for discounts for the nearby community. It is a great way to explore local restaurants and services, but will also save you some money for simply just being a student. Student discounts are huge around campuses, just be on the lookout for them! Managing your money can seem overwhelming, but with these budget apps and tips, you will be on your way to a happier bank account.

With new freedom comes new opportunities. The chance to create your own schedule is one of the best perks about college. *Scheduling Fun Fact* - Rate My Professors is a great tool to utilize when selecting your classes. There are actual student reviews of the Professor and their teaching style. Try not to stress out too much about registration. Freshman are very low on the food chain of scheduling, you just need your basic freshman classes. By my senior year, I made sure to have permanent three-day weekends, having every Friday off. Is this real life? I asked myself that multiple times during my senior year. I have to admit that it takes time to adjust to this new schedule as a freshman. You go from having your set 7 a.m. - 3 p.m. class schedule in high school to a college schedule where you could have multiple two-hour breaks within a day. It just takes time to know yourself and figure out what works best for your lifestyle.

Give yourself time to adjust to this new-found freedom. Let's be honest, it's an accomplishment in itself if you don't hit snooze three times and can remember which building your first class is located. Celebrate the small wins! Some students start class at 8 a.m. and don't have a break until 2 p.m., having back-to-back classes. This allows them to have most of their afternoon and all of their evening free. While some students prefer to sleep in and begin classes at 10 a.m., have an occasional break or two, and finish around 6 p.m. Depending on your personality, those random periods of free time can either be very productive study hours or unproductive hours spent sending GIFs to your friends back and forth. It's all about time management and creating your own structure with all of this freedom.

Don't be afraid to test out your schedule during your freshman year, you will soon find out if you are a morning or evening person. Most colleges offer evening classes for those night owls out there! The struggle can actually be real to stay awake during night classes. If you can fight the urge to not fall asleep, I applaud you. Summer classes are always an option as well if you need to catch up, retake a class, or simply want to get ahead for the upcoming year. The secret about summer classes are that they are typically smaller in size, allowing you to have a more interactive class environment, and most of the time classes finish up early (you didn't hear that from me).

For financial aid advice, utilize your high school Guidance Counselor or Academic Advisor. They will be able to provide support and guidance in this category. Once you have accepted your choice for college, you will also be assigned an Academic Advisor. They will be able to provide you with deadlines for financial aid and all things scholarships. Start to become familiar with FAFSA, the free application college students use to determine their eligibility for financial aid, loans, grants, and work-study programs. Mark your calendars and don't miss out on these important submission dates, they are crucial to your future.

During your senior year of high school and the summer before you begin college, be on the lookout for the boatload of scholarships available to you. You may not realize this, but there are scholarships for about anything. I've found that scholarships are not one size fits all. Use your own unique traits to land yourself some cash money. For your amusement, here are some scholarships I found just browsing the web. For all of you who may not be playing professional college basketball, but have height on your side, you can apply for the "Tall Clubs" scholarship. Where are my hipsters out there? There's the "Stuck at Prom" scholarship, awarded to individuals each year for designing your prom dress made out of duct tape. I mean I am talking $3,000 for dressing in duct tape that would pay for your books and more for an entire year. Start taping, ladies! Have you always been annoyed with smudging your papers due to being left-handed? All those years of smudging your paper will be worth it to be awarded the exclusive "Left-Handed" scholarship. My point is that there are so many scholarships out there. It will just take some research and an application to put you in the running!

LESSON #14

Sneak Peek Into
What Is Ahead

Within a few short months, I'm sure you will be going, "Emily, I feel like I'm owning my freshman year, now what?" First off, I want you to know that there are going to be SO many more exciting opportunities ahead of you, just be ready to take it all in. Below are some common freshman questions regarding all things future from housing to studying abroad to internships to becoming a RA to on campus jobs. Whew! I am pretty sure I've got you covered! Let's take a sneak peek into what's ahead…

Off Campus/Sorority Housing/Commuting/Car

Typically, most freshmen and even sophomores choose to live on campus for multiple reasons: great community of friends, convenient location, safe environment, and can you say all you can eat meal plan? There are some instances, depending on your situation, where you may either choose to live off campus, in sorority housing, or commute. For sorority housing, typically, you can't live in the house until at least your sophomore year. My personal advice would be to try and stay on campus as long as you can! Save those off campus experiences for when you are an upperclassman. You will have a much better understanding of the college scene and can handle more responsibilities. I promise you that you won't want to be messing with your broken faucet or clogged shower during your freshman year. You will have other things to worry about!

Let's touch on an issue that can be a common argument with the parents before you head off to school - to bring or not to bring your car to campus. I know you may disagree with me but I promise you that you will not need your car your freshman year. Everything is there for you on campus within walking distance including your classes, workout facility, friends, cafeteria, and your favorite coffee shop before those lovely 8 a.m. classes. The only bus that you'll be on is the *struggle* bus if you don't make time in your schedule to get to your classes. Hey, some colleges even have shuttles to and from your local Target or grocery store. My campus even offered Zipcars to rent when needed. How genius and affordable! I guarantee you that one of your friends will have a car for you to use for an emergency or for that much needed caffeine trip. I know the thought sounds horrible of not having access to your car on campus, but I promise you that you will be okay. Why would you want to leave your campus that has practically everything minutes away?

So, when will you need a car on campus? When you move off campus, as an upperclassman, I recommend having your car to get to and from classes and wherever else you need to go! Other than that, I don't see it necessary to have your car on campus your freshman year, it will honestly be a hassle just trying to find a parking space every day. Did I mention most colleges have freshmen parking lots that are basically located back in your hometown? By listening to these tips, you will be saving a lot of gas and money (cha-ching)!

Studying Abroad – A Whole New World

Can we just skip to the part in college where I get to travel the world? Where to start? That one time I was ziplining through New Zealand, or cruising thirteen countries on Semester at Sea, or trying every type of gelato in Italy, or the time I spent riding donkeys through Greece. Oh the memories! Sorry to say, but unfortunately the only gelato I was eating was in our town circle and the closest thing I saw to a donkey was my Uncle's large dog over the holidays. If you can't tell, the one regret that I had in college was not getting the chance to study abroad. For my personal situation, it just didn't work out for my schedule. I knew that since I jumped around colleges so much, studying abroad for an entire semester just wasn't going to be a lesson in my book. You know though, I had so many other great experiences with moving to the West Coast, that I kind of felt like I had my own adventure with the move alone. From what I have heard from peers, studying abroad is a must and can be pretty affordable at most colleges. Since I'm not an expert in this field, I decided to phone a friend, or more like email a friend, to get the real scoop on why students have fallen in love with studying abroad. Take it away, Maggie!

Where to even begin? Although studying abroad is not for everyone, I constantly encourage college students to at least look into it. There are often times more opportunities than we think and there is a country or an experience that will match your personality and courage. Whether it's studying abroad in Canada, just across the American border, or all the way down under, fifteen hours from home, the experiences, the knowledge, and the memories you gain will be entirely worth the time and money spent.

Often times I hear excuses about finances, semester schedules, and the distance. To me, those are just easy ways out. When it comes to finances, a majority of the universities you will attend will offer study abroad for the same price as in-state tuition. When it comes to semester schedules, I'm a firm believer that the broadening of your horizons outweighs graduating on time. You can also look into summer study abroad programs that won't take away from your four-year schedule. And when it comes to distance, this is one of the only opportunities you can spend a couple months with your closest college buddies, IN A DIFFERENT COUNTRY, and know that you will be coming home in the end. There are many options of where you can go. If distance is too hard for you to conquer, as I mentioned before, there are opportunities in Canada, in South America, in the Caribbean, and more. You don't always have to go across the pond for these experiences (even though I encourage you to look into those opportunities as well).

Studying abroad takes you outside your comfort zone and shows you just how small we are in comparison to this big world. It's a humbling, crazy adventure that will most likely leave you with friends all over the globe and memories that you can't make at home.

So Many Internships, So Little Time

I don't know about everyone else's experience but I felt like around day number two of my freshman year of college, people were already asking me where I am going to intern? Have you applied anywhere yet? How many internships are you going to have in college? Okay, I may be a bit dramatic (again) but I definitely felt that pressure within the first two years of college. Now, please remember that I am a big advocate of internships…they led me to a fantastic career opportunity after college. I just think that it is important to remember this piece of advice from my personal experience when it comes to internships - *quality vs. quantity*. I vividly remember sitting in a sorority chapter meeting and having a guest speaker come in to discuss her thoughts on internships as a college graduate. We all pretty much left feeling hopeless, unmotivated, and wondering how are we ever going to get to our dream job without at least having a new internship every semester. Again, emphasis on *quality over quantity*.

I began looking for my first internship, let's call it *Hunger Games* edition, during my junior year of college. Now, if the right internship comes your way freshman or sophomore year, I highly recommend taking that opportunity if your schedule allows it. For me personally, I spent the first two years, 1) switching colleges and 2) making connections to my new college (getting involved, making friends, keeping up my grades, etc.). When my junior year came along, I knew I needed to start the "hunt" for this so-called perfect internship. I had a friend reach out about doing an unpaid internship for college credit during my junior spring semester. It was at a local event company only about thirty minutes away from campus and at the time, I was all about becoming an event planner. Long story short, my so-called perfect looking internship on the outside turned out to be one of the worst first experiences as an intern. By the end of the internship, I had done very little event planning and basically ran errands for one of the owners. When I say errands, I mean getting coffee EVERY morning, taking a VERY expensive car to get a carwash and oil change, and my personal favorite, going to return a pair of pants at a very upscale department store with no receipt. I knew this was how a "typical" intern was portrayed in the movies, but now I am empowered to know that this is not always the case and I am capable of much more than being their personal barista or car mechanic.

My second internship led me to a local, trendy, and empowering organization with a staff of about ten called 31 Bits (highly recommend checking them out). The company had a powerful mission of impacting the lives of women in Uganda (see, that was my first step in saving the world), by using fashion and design to empower people to rise above poverty. This time, I took a different approach and worked as their Sales & Administration intern. I basically packaged their jewelry and shipped them to their customers, but I truly enjoyed the overall experience. My final and most important internship was one that I had to be turned down ELEVEN times to truly realize the importance of working hard to get to where you want to be. Those eleven declines pushed me harder than ever during my senior year of college. I was graduating early and had only one company on my mind. Within weeks of finishing, I had two phone interviews, had been flown to their headquarters, and completed an in-person interview in front of a panel of four. I am honored to say that I became a Culture Services intern (my dream internship) for a major airline company that led me to my first full time job after college. Now, every internship experience is going to be unique, but I came up with a few tips for any career path. Good luck and happy interning!

Top 5 Internship Tips:

1. **Dream big.**

   No internship is ever "out of your league." If you want to be an intern at a Fortune 500 Company, work at your favorite non-profit organization, or for your dream television show, you can do it. I'll be your biggest fan. Just place your focus on intentional college experiences and work/organizations that will prepare you to apply for that dream internship.

2. **Utilize your campus career center.**

   It may seem daunting to bring your resume in for someone to critique and discuss the different options you have, but that is the sole reason why campus career centers exist. They know the ins and outs of all things internships. Don't be afraid to use them! Oh, and did I mention that these centers have connections to about every internship in the area from previous students? I don't know about you, but I'm sold on campus career centers.

3. **Use internships as a test trial.**

   Every internship is a learning experience. Remember that taking an internship is not the end of the world if it doesn't turn out to be your favorite or what you thought it would be. That is what the internship process is all about! This is the time to figure out what you like about work environments, what schedule you prefer, and it gives the unique opportunity to try out a potential full time career move. Utilize every internship as a guide to hopefully find your ideal job after college.

4. **Be creative.**
During my internship application process for my dream internship, before entering the real world, I went around on airplanes with a book that I made asking their employees what they love so much about working for that company. I took that book filled with quotes and signatures from employees all over the country to my interview and they still ask about that book today. It can work in virtually any industry, it just so happened that mine was during my trips on an airplane. Think outside the box!

5. **Work hard, play hard!**
Internships are a lot of hard work, but I always tried to have a little fun while at the job. Whether being able to fly

for free on the weekends or having the opportunity to go paddle boarding as a team outing, you can always find a little fun out there in the sometimes intimidating "real world." Keep in mind that internships are stepping stones to landing your first job after college, so work hard, show up on time, and be productive. A strong recommendation letter from a previous boss can go a long way!

Life of a Resident Assistant

Something to think about for your future, being a RA is a highly sought out position after your freshman year of college. To tell you a little bit more, let's hear from an expert who has been one herself. Oh, and she just so happens to be my sweet sister-in-law, Amber!

There are numerous benefits to being a RA. I applied to be a RA for several reasons...

1. *I did not feel that I was challenging myself enough and needed to get out of my comfort zone.*

2. *I was thinking about a career in higher education.*
3. *I was extremely grateful that my parents were paying for my education and felt the need to also contribute (the compensation for being a RA at my college was tuition).*

That being said, applying to be a RA was one of the best decisions I ever made. I met new people, learned to balance my responsibilities in the residence halls with schoolwork, learned how to approach and deal with difficult situations, and was challenged every single day.

Being a RA is not a walk in the park and is a huge commitment, so if you are only seeing the 'free tuition' part of the job description, the job is not for you. As a RA, you're committed to pretty much being a RA and going to class. That's it. You forgo a lot of your free time with friends to plan events, hang out with your residents, make bulletin boards, and of course, do your schoolwork!

The job of a RA is challenging, frustrating, fun, and extremely rewarding, all at the same time. That being said, there are also very serious issues a RA deals with that should not be taken lightly.

I have dealt with issues, or known RAs, whom have had issues with roommate disputes, extreme homesickness, underage drinking, residents struggling with eating disorders, death of a parent, and rape; so the job is not to be taken lightly. While these issues happen on rare occasions, it is to be expected that as a RA, you will encounter challenging situations.

On the lighter side, I did have loads of fun planning programs, working with other RAs, and enjoying late night conversations with residents while doing nightly rounds. The rewards that I reaped from being a RA by far outweighed the troubles and I ended up learning so much about myself and my capabilities.

Anyone looking to get outside of his or her comfort zone, gain valuable experiences that can be applied to almost any career field, and is not afraid to dedicate a lot of time to the job, should definitely look into the amazing opportunity of being a Resident Assistant.

Work, Work, Work, Work, Work

Insert Rihanna's "Work" chorus here. I highly recommend trying to find an on campus job, if at all possible. This can be a great option, especially when juniors and seniors. If you may not have the schedule for an internship, finding a job on campus is a great solution. It is super convenient, fun, and may even bring in some money for that cute romper you've been eyeing. Another added bonus is that the majority of the time, the employer will work around your class schedule since you are working for the college. They realize that your education is the priority and working is just an added plus. I also know that most colleges tend to need help in the library. You may be thinking, really Emily…the library? Just hear me out, most of the time you finish up your work early and can spend the rest of your time studying (double bonus). Did I mention cute guys also frequent the library? Whether working for the Athletic Department, giving campus tours for Admissions, or organizing books in the school library, finding a job on campus has its benefits!

For those of you who are planning on working at an off campus job while juggling everything else going on in your life, I first of all applaud you. You will quickly realize that you will have to create a schedule to make sure you stay on top of your schoolwork, social life, and overall well-being. Oh, and did I mention sleep? Working while in college can be very overwhelming, but also rewarding. My advice would be to try and select a job that you are interested in or may help in your future career goals. It's a win-win if you find a job that also aligns with your passion.

LESSON #15

Friends That Walked the Path

What is one piece of advice that you would tell your college self? Who better to hear from than women who have walked the path? When talking to friends from all different states and colleges about our "glory" years, I knew they had more to share. So, I decided to ask a range of young women, who attended all different size colleges, in different states, their perspective of college. What I really wanted to know was what piece of advice they would have told their college self today. Let's take a sneak peek into the experiences of fifteen dear friends of mine who want to be there for you, too.

Try not to grow up too quickly. Focus on school, family, friends, and what makes you happy... Everything else will fall into place. – Janie K.

During our various climbs in life, we will cross paths with many different people. We will have some climbing partners who will walk alongside us for thousands of miles and some only several yards. Each person will serve a different purpose in our journey, as we will in theirs. But the majority of the trek will consist of long hauls and stretches of land that we will have to conquer on our own. The only person who will be with you one hundred percent of the time, from your first step to your last, is YOU. Make the effort to get to know yourself, to become your own best friend. Adore yourself; learn what makes you feel whole without the influence of another. CELEBRATE YOURSELF because you are worth that extra mile. – Camellia

If you are religious, find a friend whose faith is also important to them, and decide to go to church together every week. This makes it a lot easier to keep faith a part of your life when you're in a world where it's so easy to lose. You'll find that you can keep each other both accountable and company! – Ava

Take time for yourself. One thing society neglects to teach us is the importance of self-reflection. We constantly surround ourselves with people, television shows, and social media apps. Find the solitude in solo coffee dates, in late night journaling, in the current New York Times best seller, in yoga at your favorite studio, in any and all things that bring you back to yourself and your center. As much as I believe in building strong friendships and a core community, at the end of the day you are the last person you speak to. Make sure what you're saying to yourself is positive, loving, and accurate. If you can do this, you can do anything you put your mind to, because you will be your biggest fan. – Maggie

Just say it. Say what's on your mind; be honest with how you feel. It's okay to be you and put yourself out there. You'll be rewarded and feel liberated for saying what's true to you. It took me four years of college to learn that, but by my senior year, I lived it, and I've never felt better. – Mandi

Stay true to yourself and follow your passions. It may feel like you have to do everything your peers are doing, but I promise after graduation, that won't matter. It's cheesy, but the saying, "those who mind don't matter, and those who matter don't mind" is absolutely correct! – Kelsea

My four pieces of advice: 1) Study abroad anywhere! 2) Do internships in different professional fields so you get the opportunity to try different things. That opportunity goes away after college! Try to do at least three internships. 3) Don't take college too seriously! It may seem like it's a big deal in the moment, but all you need to do is graduate. Don't fret the small things. 4) College is the first time you're picking your friends as an adult. Try to choose people you enjoy spending time with and not necessarily the people you wish you could be. – Megan

It's so important to remember who you are, what your values are, and what you believe. Everything you've known to be true will either be challenged, stretched or affirmed by both your Professors and your friends. And that's a big part of why you go to college – to grow, change and learn to critically think about how you view the world. Remember that you don't have to assimilate to what others are doing or how they're thinking; your job is to actively take it all in and evaluate your own beliefs and values and the views of those around you and hopefully come to your own understanding of the world with a newfound depth and richness. – Mallory

It's okay to not know how everything is going to work out, just as long as you keep moving. Expect the unexpected. It makes things more fun and less stressful. – Brittnei

1. Don't wear slippery shoes on a first date. Trust me. 2. Surround yourself with people who both allow and challenge you to be your best, most authentic self. Don't expect to find them right away, but when you do – keep them around. 3. Find time to be outside. 4. Find an activity that

rejuvenates you and make it a practice. It doesn't matter if it's yoga, reading, journaling, walking, sitting outside, or spending time with a good friend. Find something that brings you peace and joy and make it a part of your routine. 5. Get involved. Freshman year is the perfect time to get involved in as many clubs and organizations as possible. They are a great way to meet people, get involved on campus, and gain interesting experiences to add to your resume and talk about in interviews. You can always pick and choose what you are passionate about, but make sure you explore your options and try lots of new things. 6. Don't forget to call your parents. They really miss you and would love to hear how things are going. 7. Get to know your Professors. They are smart, interesting people with lots of life experience. Take advantage of office hours with Professors who inspire you. Professors are helpful for more than just improving your grades. They are great mentors who can help you discover interesting career paths, and they are some of the best advocates when it comes to applying for jobs. A strong, personal recommendation letter can go a long way. – Marnie

Experiences are always more important than money, so do not worry about finances! Study abroad, take the unpaid internship, and go on Spring Break, because after school is over, you'll have a job, limited vacation time, and bills. – Amber

If there's one thing that college taught me, it's not to take yourself too seriously. I remember being a freshman and being so concerned about what I would wear to class, or who to talk to, or even what sorority I should join. As time went on, I realized that this was the time in my life where I could completely be myself, be weird, and say what I wanted to say (and start my own dance parties). Because of this, I made the most amazing friends that I will have the rest of life and look back on my college years without any regrets. So if anything, take these four years to be anything you want to be and don't overthink it or take it too seriously. – Jamie

Focus on you. Be the daughter, sister, friend, and person you want to be. Figure out what you are passionate about and work for it. Relationships come and go, the key is to make sure you learn

something from each of them. Do what makes you happy. Have faith in yourself. Love who you are.
– Lauren

Don't take the time spent, the people you meet, and your experience for granted. I feel like I blinked and I was graduating. I truly had the best four years of my life. Never again, will I have all of my best friends in one spot, living just minutes from each other. Never again will I live with twenty of my closest friends. Enjoy it. Don't spend so much time stressing about the little things. Looking back I spent so much of freshman year worrying. Worrying about my grades, a test, a class, a clinical. I would call my parents weekly balling telling them that I "failed" this test or that test, just to call them back a week later and tell them I got an A. Cut yourself some slack. It will all fall into place. Make time for yourself. Enjoy the time and experiences that have been given to you. If you stay organized, I promise you can manage your study schedule and have fun along the way. When I look back at my college career, it's not the C on a test that I studied so hard for and was disappointed that I remember. It's the late nights having heart-to-hearts with people I just met, it's the nights we did something so last minute and spontaneous when I should have been studying that we had the greatest time. It's the friends and the memories that I made along the way that hold my college experience so near and dear to my heart. Enjoy every minute of it, you won't regret it! – Ellen

1. Get out of your comfort zone. 2. Always say yes to late night pizza. When else in your life is it acceptable to eat greasy cheap pizza? Take advantage of your metabolism while you can! 3. Check before you send an email response to your Professor or entire class. "Reply All" can be tricky. 4. The frat guy you thought you liked. Think again. 5. Always be yourself. – Ali

Victory Lap

She will fly. She will be independent. She will conquer mountains. She will leave a positive mark in society. She will start her own dance parties. She will laugh at her own jokes. She will be a leader. She will be a role model. She will be proud of her accomplishments. She will make her own steps to creating a better world. She will have faith. She will say yes to adventure. She will embrace change. She will define her own destiny. She will…

Everyone deserves that final victory lap, right? I can see the finish line, but I'm not ready to give you amazing ladies up just yet! What do

I see in the future for you? I imagine you at the start line, about to take off, but not fully ready to all out sprint (I'm tired just thinking about it). You may be nervous, curious, and scared of the unknown ahead of you and *that is okay*. I completely understand. What I want you to be – excited, optimistic, and ready to take on the world of college! My hope for you is this, to shed those freshman fifteen fears and enjoy some of the best years of your life.

Can I tag along? I'll be like your wingwoman...but for college. I want to see your first day of college photos, outfits, planners, dorm rooms, embarrassing moments, killing it at orientation, and your "she is more" moments! Follow and tag me on Instagram @shewholeads and hashtag #freshmanfifteen to follow along the thousands of other women who are just like you! As much as I would love for you to just "follow me," my ultimate goal is for you to *co-lead* with me. Let's create a forum for inspiration, love, and support! Freshman year can be intimidating, but I say, let's conquer it together! Ask me questions, leave comments, and spread the love. Oh and please don't forget, have a little fun on that victory lap!

**She is more than the freshman fifteen
and you will be, too!**

Interested in hearing more from Emily? She is more...than just an author, she is also available for speaking engagements on a number of inspirational topics. Please reach out to heppemily@gmail.com for more information!

CPSIA information can be obtained
at www.ICGtesting.com
Printed in the USA
LVOW07s0306260517
535914LV00001B/2/P

9 781478 787396